LEEDS 2

in the Fifties, Sixties and Seventies

vol. **2**

YORKSHIRE
Evening Post

LEEDS
in the Fifties, Sixties and Seventies

vol. 2

DB
PUBLISHING

First published in Great Britain in 2010 by The Derby Books Publishing
Company Limited, 3 The Parker Centre, Derby, DE21 4SZ

All the photographs in this book are available to buy from the *Evening Post's*
Photosales website at **www.photostoday.co.uk**

ISBN 978-1-85983-875-4

Printed and bound by Rzeszowskie Zaklady Graficzne S.A. Poland.

Contents

Foreword

THE photographs from the archives of the *Yorkshire Evening Post* brought together in this book tell the story of a changing Leeds. We may recognise the shape of many of the buildings, we may have walked down the streets featured, we may even know some of the people pictured – you could even be one of those people – but the city shown is not the city of today.

Leeds in these photographs, especially the older photographs from the 1950s, is a city where memories of a World War were still fresh, where heavy industry still employed tens of thousands of workers and home for most was built of red brick. Many of the large buildings and factories now exist only in photographs, having been cleared to make way for new workplaces and new homes. One of the roads shown often in these pages is Wellington Street, now home to the *Yorkshire Evening Post* – many of the shops and offices here during those post-war decades are long gone.

The links between the lives we have now and the lives of these past years, though, are strong. It is clear from the photographs that people in the fifties, sixties and seventies were as used as we are today to seeing old buildings demolished and new ones appear.

Crowds queuing for tickets at Elland Road are hardly a modern phenomenon and foot and mouth brought problems in the 1960s, just as it has in Yorkshire in recent years. There are also a few familiar faces – look out especially for a young Denis Healey just returned from a visit down a pit and a very fresh-faced Jack Straw dancing at a student ball. There are many photographs in this book of children. There are children at play and children at school. These Leeds children are the parents and grandparents of young people in Leeds today.

Our first book of photographs of Leeds in the fifties, sixties and seventies was warmly received and greatly enjoyed. For many, the photographs shown helped blow the dust off memories of a childhood nearly a lifetime ago.

I hope you enjoy this second volume of photographs of the recent past of our great city.

Paul Napier
Editor
Yorkshire Evening Post

The 1950s

Passengers line a platform at Leeds City Station as a train approaches from Glasgow for London, 31 May 1955.

Joe Davis in action at the People's Hall, where he is playing a five-day series with Willie Smith on 23 September 1950.

The Earl of Harewood and his six-year-old son Mark blow on the bamboo pipes before a performance at Harewood House of 'Signals for Solo Clarinet and Electronic Sounds' on 1 March 1951.

Also pictured are the Countess of Harewood and the composer of this work Harrison Birtwistle.

The 1951 General Election on 26 October 1951. The scene inside Leeds Town Hall – rows and rows of tables and a large body of counters totalling the votes cast in the different consituences.

People line up to be vaccinated in Danube Grove, Geldered Road, on 14 April 1953. It is not known what the vaccination was for.

ARMOUR COUNTS—

but men count most!

Britain is building up her armour—and armour, as even King Arthur knew, is a dead loss without a knight inside it! From now on many more men will be needed. Men good enough to hold a position and win promotion in this permanent, highly specialised team of crack combat units—The Regular Army. Have you got what it takes—the brains to master technical weapons, the tough good-humoured character that can learn to obey and command? You have? Then find out what the New Deal for Regular Army men can now offer *you* in pay and prospects. Call today at a recruiting office, or post the coupon below.

There's room for the best today in the

REGULAR ARMY

The War Office ·AG10/35· London · SW1 *Please send me without obligation, the new fully illustrated book 'The Regular Army', and details of increased pay.*

Name_____ Age_____

Address _____

Old adverts from the *Yorkshire Evening Post*, 1951: ARMY ADVERT. BRISTOL STREET MOTORS.

Look to *BUSH* for Television satisfaction

MODEL TV.22

49 GNS.
(TAX PAID)

Everything in this Bush model TV.22, both seen and unseen, is designed to bring you lasting television satisfaction. The clarity of the picture, the shapeliness of the cabinet, the famous Bush reliability—all of these have been combined at a price which ensures real value for money. Every Bush set is the product of nearly twenty years' experience and skill in the manufacture of television. Ask your Bush dealer to show you the TV.22—you, too, will be enthusiastic when you see what a fine model it is.

BRILLIANT PICTURES

ONLY TWO CONTROLS
for normal use.

OPERATES on A.C. or D.C.

SPECIAL CIRCUITS
check interference.

SUITABLE TO ANY B.B.C.
Television transmitter.

BUSH TELEVISION
BUSH RADIO LTD., POWER ROAD, CHISWICK, W.4

reyds T51/11/8

An old MABANES advert from the *Yorkshire Evening Post*, 1952.

An old BUSH TELEVISION advert from the *Yorkshire Evening Post*, 1951.

An old GOBLIN ELECTRIC WASHING MACHINES advert from the *Yorkshire Evening Post*, 1952.

An old MILLETTS advert from the *Yorkshire Evening Post*, 1951.

Leeds Fire Brigade has taken delivery of three new Rolls-Dennis fire engines, the first peacetime additions since before the war, on 12 October 1953. Two more arrived shortly after. They are the latest design and pump 625 gallons a minute at 100lb pressure. The machines have a turning circle of less that 30ft. They replace machines going out of service.

Coal Staithes, February 1954.

Two librarians in the newly opened Law Library in the Town Hall, February 1955.

Members of Leeds Amateur Radio Society with their low-power receiver and transmitter, 1 March 1955.

Prefabs in Crossfield Street, St Mark's Estate, Woodhouse Lane on 13 October 1955.

The Empire Theatre, 26 October 1955. Arthur Askey registers amazement at the size of his garment after his daughter Anthea has shrunk it in the wash. The Askeys are appearing in *The Love Match* at the Empire Theatre this week.

Opposite: Mr Denis Winston Healey, Socialist MP for East Leeds, visited part of his constituency 639ft under the ground on 27 September 1956. Our picture shows Mr Healey (left) at Waterloo Main Colliery with Mr Vollans and Mr Firth. Mr Healey (39), who weighs 13 and a half stone and is over 6ft tall, at one stage crawled 70yds on his stomach in a space 2ft 5in high to talk to constituents.

He was making his second visit to Waterloo Main Colliery, which lies within Leeds City boundary. He last made the 50-second descent a year ago and explained 'There's no political significance about my visits. I'm not conducting an underground movement. I just want to get to know as much as possible about conditions here, and to meet some of my constituents on the job.'

He had not gone into training for the visit which entailed a 20-minute walk to the coal face.

'I don't train beforehand – I convalesce afterwards,' he said.

Wearing a size 7 and 3 eighths helmet, blue overalls and knee pads, and carrying the traditional yardstick, Mr Healey was accompanied by the pit manager, Mr F. Vollans, the safety officer, Mr G.W. Firth who has worked at the pit since 1919, Mr Walter McDonough, secretary of Waterloo Main branch of the NUM and the branch president, Mr T. Hunt.

Each carried a gas detecting flame lamp to light the way along the labyrinth of workings, which are electrically lighted only at the junctions.

Mr Firth said 'The miners really appreciate Mr Healey's personal interest in what goes on down below.'

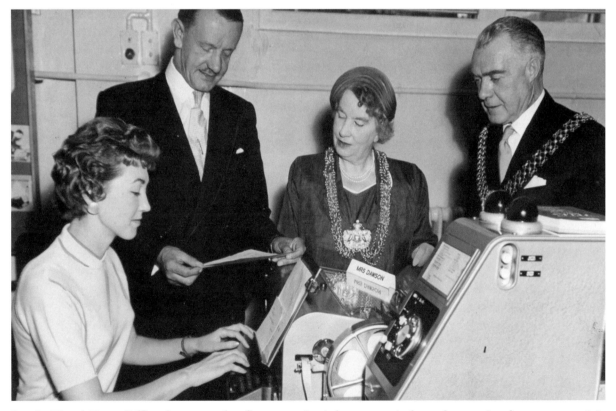

Leeds Head Post Office became the first provincial auto-switch exchange in the country. Mr Kenneth Thompson, MP, the Assistant Postmaster General (left), with Alderman Mrs Mary Pearce (Lord Mayor of Leeds) and Alderman N.N. Durrant (Lord Mayor of Bradford) watch Mrs Jean Dawson send a message during the opening ceremony of the new telex exchange at Leeds Head Post Office, 1 September 1958.

The Redhaw family, of Sandhill Lane, Moortown, at work again on 1 November 1958 with their annual effort for the *Evening Post* Toy Appeal. They set up a stall outside the Post Office at Moortown, selling books, sweets and fancy goods. Standing by the stall are (left to right) Martin Redshaw (15), Mrs R.B. Redshaw and Digby (10).

Park Row, the Prudential Assurance Building, 4 November 1958.

Here is the new look in sidecars for RAC patrolmen – seen in Leeds on 5 October 1959 for the first time. It is a completely new design, with much more streamlining than the old-style box.

1958
Gaillac s/Tarn
Kristianstad
Laon
Rennes
L'Aigle
Le Bourget
Mende
Nantes
Coventry
Bourg en Bresse
Freigné

LEON BIANCOTTO

Record du monde de Vol Inverse 1"16
Cormeilles-Pontoise 14-5-1957
des Coupes Internationales de Voltige Aérienne
1956-1958

Yeadon, Leeds Bradford Airport, 18 May 1959. On more than one occaision Leon Biancotto came to Yeadon to give daring shows, including flying upside down a few feet from the deck. He was tragically killed on a practice flight.

Mr Macmillan raises his hand to emphasise a point in his speech to a large crowd outside Leeds Town hall on 30 September 1959.

The recently completed roundabout at West Park on Otley Road on 18 December 1958.

The 1960s

View of the centre of Leeds in the 1960s looking towards Armley. The city campus of Leeds College of Technology is on the left with Leeds Town Hall and the Civic Hall in the background.

City of Leeds Cleansing Department, 25 January 1960.

Yeadon, 27 January 1960. The new fire-fighting and rescue vehicles, valued at about £7,000, which have been delivered to the Leeds-Bradford Airport as part of the Leeds and Bradford Joint Aerodrome Committee's scheme to improve the airport's facilities, efficiency and safety measures. The fire engine is the most modern of its type in the country, being specially designed for airfield work. Included in its equipment is an automatic foam unit capable of smothering aircraft fores. Its attendant rescue vehicle has its own generator for powering search lights, saws, and other equipment. It is fitted with radio and can be directed from the airport's control tower.

Residents in the Duxbury Street (Camp Road) area of Leeds queueing to enter the mass radiography mobile unit, run by the Leeds Regional Hospital Board, which was touring the district holding street sessions, on 20 July 1960.

Printing presses in operation in the modern factory at Seacroft on 15 July 1960. Beck and Inchbold Ltd, of Seacroft, Leeds, one of the leading printing businesses in the North of England, has its beginnings when Thomas Inchbold was apprenticed to a Leeds bookseller in 1800.

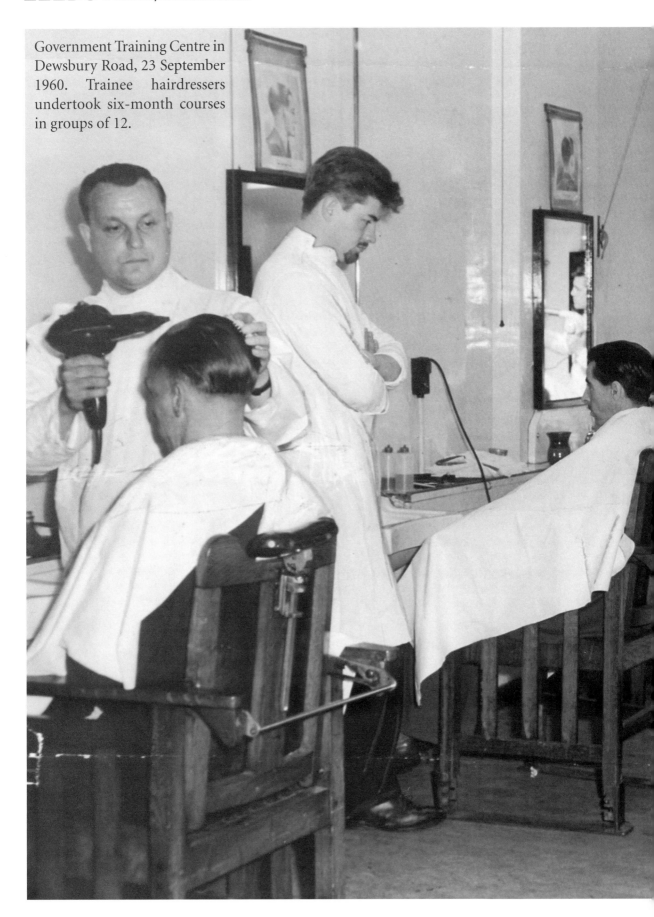

Government Training Centre in Dewsbury Road, 23 September 1960. Trainee hairdressers undertook six-month courses in groups of 12.

Obituary from 12 January 1961: 'Mr Herbert Dewhirst, former *Evening Post* photographer, who, during a 50-year long Press career with his camera, captured in pictures major national, international and local events, has died in hospital in Lancaster. He was 73. His career began in the years of the suffragettes, with camera flashes created from dollops of magnesium powder ignited in a tray. In World War One he and his cameras served with the Royal Flying Corps and in World War Two he was a front line flying photographer. He had photographed every Prime Minister since Asquith and his war pictures, including those he took when he landed in France on D-Day and during the subsequent conquest of the Nazis, were published in newspapers all over the world.'

Councillor Mrs May Sexton chats with two boys among houses in Apsley Street, 22 August 1961.

Leeds Corporation bus drivers in 1961. A party of officials and drivers of Leeds Corporation Transport Depatment, who had been delivering buses for use in London, had had an accident at Grantham the previous afternoon. Seven or eight in number, they were returning in a Leeds Corporation van, which collided with a lorry and was overturned. The following officials and drivers were either uninjured or sustained minor injuries: Harry Woodhouse, Harry Horne, Ralph Webster, Arthur Starkey, George Meredith, James Isles and C. Macauley.

Included in this picture are: E. Taylor (background), fitter. A. Sheerman, bodybuilder. L. Halstead (Slem), fitter. R. Allen, foreman. A. Croft, electrician. J. Lavell, foreman. A. Starkey, foreman. J. Barkley, fitter.

An 1891 model of the Samson Steam fire engine, which had 60 years of operational life, was brought into action again on 7 September 1961 at the Leeds Eastern Fire Station. The machine, which was formerly kept at Harewood House and later at Goldsborough Hall, was acquired recently by Leeds Fire Brigade.

View of Armley from above from 13 October 1962 showing bus depot, terraced streets, power station and chimneys.

Photograph dated 10 October 1963. The Leeds firm of wine merchants, T.P. Mallorie and Co. Ltd, which has a history going back 151 years was taken over by Holt Sons and Co. Ltd, India Buildings, Liverpool.

Outside of Leeds Central Station from
Station Approach on 27 August 1963.

8/6 weekly rents
The Official Granada TV Set.

(The set that's too good to buy.)

This precision instrument was specially designed for Red Arrow by Granada's
own engineers. (And who knows more about television than Granada?) It's
built to give a vivid, bright picture, with no glare. And its sound-system
reproduces words *and* music clear as a bell.

Our powerful aerial helps good reception, too. We designed it to scoop the complete picture out of the air and send it, undistorted, down to your set. You'll see.

We keep your set in perfect condition, free, forever. We hate to have it
even *flicker*. And we never, never leave you without a set.

To prove all this we'll lend you one—free—for 10 days. If you decide not to
keep it, we won't be annoyed. Just surprised. 19" set. 8/6 weekly for a year
(minimum period). £6.7.6. initial deposit.

RED ARROW
(GRANADA'S TV RENTAL SERVICE)

Red Arrow showroom at 19 Boar Lane, Leeds Tel. 35594 (also in Leeds at Armley, Crossgates,
and Kirkstall Rd.). Other showrooms in: Barnsley · Bradford · Brighouse · Dewsbury
Doncaster · Halifax · Huddersfield · Morley · Ripon.

Old advert for Granada from the
Yorkshire Evening Post, 1964.

IT'S THE MAN THAT'S IMPORTANT IN DORMAN LONG

Men from Dorman Long travel the world securing orders for steel, for steel bridges, for multi-storey and other buildings to be erected in structural steel-work. The skills which have been perfected over the years in the company's works thus become monuments of British engineering technology in many parts of the globe. Thousands of tons of steel are exported in this way to the benefit of the whole community. Every man in Dorman Long—from manager to apprentice—is contributing to the nation's prosperity.

This is personal achievement at its best—Nationalisation cramps the individual.

DORMAN LONG · Middlesbrough · Makers of steel — builders of bridges

Old advert for Dorman Long from the *Yorkshire Evening Post*, 1964.

Record queues at Leeds United's Elland Road ground formed in 1964 when tickets for the 25 January FA Cup tie with Everton went on sale. Football fans and, in many cases, their wives began queueing at 6am – three hours before selling United's share of the 50,000 tickets began.

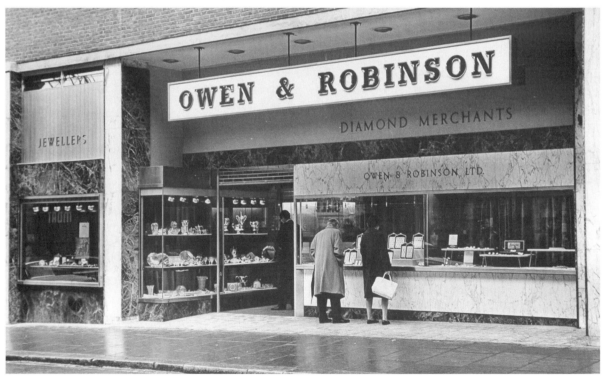

The attractive frontage of Owen & Robinson's new shop in Albion Street in May 1964 with the display windows and entrance set back undercover.

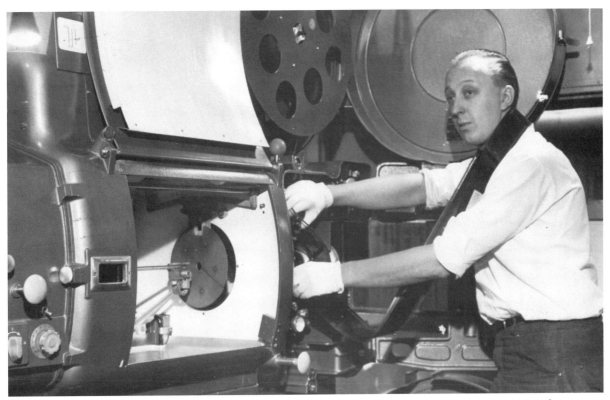

In a room packed with over £10,000 worth of electronic equipment on 10 August 1964, four men in white coats and gloves will supervise the screening of 52 hours of wide-screen film every week. These are the projectionists in the ultra-modern projection room at the New Odeon where *The Fall of the Roman Empire* will be screened 14 times a week. Chief projectionist is Mr Jack Lambert (pictured), chief at the Majestic for over four years. Before that he was at the Gaumont in Bradford.

Neville Street on 17 August 1964.

The Carnegie College of Physical Education at Beckett Park, Leeds on 20 October 1964. This is the impressive exterior of the new gymnasium which is shared by students of Carnegie College and Leeds Training College.

Old advert for Capstan Cigarettes from the *Yorkshire Evening Post*, 1965.

Old advert for Co-Op Camera Shop from the *Yorkshire Evening Post*, 1965.

Leathley Lane, Autowreckers Ltd, Mr Brian Swales, the firm's transport manager, on 2 September 1965.

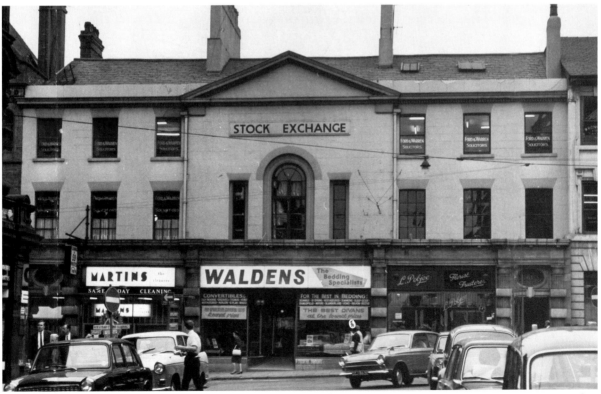

Leeds Stock Exchange in October 1966, which stood with its desecrated Georgian front facing down Albion Place.

Elland Road on 30 April 1965. Rubble adjoining Mr Dobson's garage and derelict property alongside the trim houses in Baron Close. Mr G. Dobson, garage proprietor, of Elland Road threatened legal action in letters to the city's Public Health Department and the Town Clerk alleging that the Corporation was responsible for derelict property adjoining and near his home.

Down comes another Leeds building, this time at the corner of St Paul's Street and East Parade. In the background is the Town Hall, 2 March 1966.

Leeds, 1 August 1966. It has been estimated that a 10 per cent reduction of pollution in the River Aire at Leeds would bring many kinds of fish back. In this part of the Leeds and Liverpool Canal system, near Whitehall Road, hopeful youngsters seek catches.

Leeds United Annual Meeting on 12 December 1966. 'Heads down' for a thoughtful moment at Leeds United's annual meeting. From left to right: Mr Harry Reynolds (standing), chairman; Mr Albert Morris, Mr Bob Roberts, Mr Sidney Simon, directors; Mr Cyril Williamson, general manager; Mr Don Revie, team manager. Next to Mr Reynolds on the other side is Councillor Sam Bolton, director.

Elland Road, 24 September 1966. A policeman climbs into the crowd at Elland Road on Saturday after trouble at the Leeds United v Everton game.

Old advert for Marshall & Snelgrove from the *Yorkshire Evening Post*, 1967.

Old advert for Arnold G. Wilson from the *Yorkshire Evening Post*, 1967.

The Leeds College of Commerce, 28 February 1967. Mr R.E. Hunt takes a class in the language laboratory.

Grand Theatre on 24 January 1967. 'Billy Dainty as Widow Twanky takes an admiring peep at himself in the mirror. The name Billy Dainty trips off the tongue with a degree of lightness comparable to the adroit nimbleness its owner displays on the stage. It is his real name, "A Black Country name," says Billy, flashing a toothy smile reminiscent of Bernie Winters, with whom, along with brother Mike, he has made several television appearances. Billy was born at Dudley, Worcestershire, of a non-showbusiness family, apart from mother, the dedicated amateur producer of a concert party which, in the middle thirties, was the pride and joy of the Midland Red bus company.'

Wellington Street, 1967. Bean Ing Mills, site for the new Yorkshire Post Newspapers buildings is on the left of the picture. The name on the front of the building reads 'Joshua Wilson and Sons Ltd.' The picture was taken looking down Wellington Street. The entrance to Westgate is on the right.

Looking across Leeds City Police Headquarters in March 1967 towards the Town Hall from the new swimming pool building.

Armley, 29 April 1967. Film star Jayne Mansfield pictured outside Armley Jail. Original caption: 'Jayne Mansfield and Dian Dors, two of the best known screen sex symbols, are appearing within a few miles of each other and staying at the same hotel in Wakefield this week. Jayne Mansfield arrived in Yorkshire yesterday with her famous chihuahuas

for an appearance at Armley Jail before starting a week in cabaret at Batley Varieties. She left the prison in a Rolls-Royce provided by Batley Varieties Club, accompanied by Mr. Alan Wells, owner of a country club at Weston-Super-Mare, where she was appearing last week. Jayne was wearing a low cut mini-dress, was surrounded by a crowd of retainers and friends, including Mr. Wells whom she described as "A real Gentleman". Background information: Jayne Mansfield, born 19 April 1933, was one of the leading blonde sex symbols of the 1950s and 60s. She was killed in a car crash in Biloxi, Mississippi on 29 June 1967 exactly two months after this picture in Leeds was taken.'

Pupils of Priestthorpe Seconday School, Farsley, near Leeds, use the new bridge on 22 May 1967, which has been built for them by Pudsey Council so that they can safely cross the Leeds-Bradford ring road near the school entrance.

Seacroft village green on 15 August 1967
with relics of cricket matches.

A general view of Leeds International Swiming Pool from 25 August 1967.

Seacroft, 13 December 1967. The bird's-eye view which many Seacroft people get from their lofty flats near the shopping centre – block upon block of council houses disappearing into the winter mist.

A ban on racing was imposed on 5 January 1968 to help combat the foot and mouth epidemic. 'British names – instead of French – go on to the board at a Leeds bookmakers today as racing gets underway again. Race-starved punters "faced the tapes" for the resumption of English racing today after a blank period of six weeks in which they were reduced to betting on greyhounds and computer races.'

Elland Road, 15 February 1968. Leeds United's ground staff, augmented by a gang of 90 casual workers, were at Elland Road before dawn on this day – the floodlights were switched on to assist them – clearing straw from the pitch in readiness for the afternoon's FA Cup fourth-round tie with Nottingham Forest. United had taken the precaution of spreading straw after the West Ham game. The picture shows John Reynolds (seated on roller) and Cecil Burroughs helping to put the finishing touches.

Burmantofts, 6 December 1967. A scene which might bring to mind a Brontë landscape, but for a now-abandoned three-piece suite and new flats in the mist to the right.

The Duchess of Kent dances with Mr Jack Straw, President of Leeds University Student's Union. Leeds University Student's Union, on 2 February 1968 at the annual dinner and ball.

Rodley, 23 February 1968. The swing bridge on Leeds and Liverpool canal. The boat is named *Day Dem*.

Leeds, Civic Hall, March 1968. League Cup 1967–68. Billy Bremner with Colonel and Mrs Turnbull, Lord and Lady Mayor of Leeds.

Corpus Christi Roman Catholic Secondary School. A luxury fitting? Pupils at the Corpus Christi Roman Catholic Secondary School using a telephone placed at their disposal in the school corridor on 22 March 1968.

A rubble-strewn street in the heart of Leeds on 20 March 1968.

Old furniture and bedding on wasteland at the junction of Oatland Road and Oatland Lane on 29 March 1968.

Priestley Hall in Park Row, near City Square, April 1968. Another well-known landmark in the centre of Leeds falls to the blows of the demolition men.

Leeds United supporters at Old Trafford for the FA Cup semi-final on 27 April 1968.

Leeds Bradford Airport, 15 June 1968. Enrico Tomasso (7) greets Louis Armstrong with a tune on his trumpet – and the great Satchmo listens critically.

Louis Armstrong and the All Stars were appearing at Batley Variety Club.

Regent Street flyover, 11 May 1968. Crane jib strikes Leeds Corporation bus. 'Before the crane jib struck the bus, two independent witnesses had seen it leaning, but told no one about it,' Mr Leonard Wilman, prosecuting for HM Inspector of Factories, told the Leeds Stipendiary Magistrate, Mr John Randolph. The owners of the crane, Alphapile Ltd, City Road, Derby, pleaded guilty on the behalf on Mr Christopher Holland for failing to ensure the stablility of a lifting appliance, and were fined £100.

Spenceley Street, 29 June 1968.

Selby Road and York Road junction, 29 June 1968.

Roundhay, 23 July 1968. Falling under the demolition men's hammers was Harehill's Cinema on Roundhay Road, together with adjoining property. The site was to be redeveloped as a shopping area.

Seacroft tower blocks, 7 October 1968.

19 July 1968. As old buildings are being demolished, new views of the city and its buildings are constantly being opened up. One of the latest 'new looks' is from outside the Civic Theatre in Cookridge Street looking across the demolition site of the former Cookridge Street Baths towards the Civic Hall and the Brotherton Wing of Leeds General Infirmary. The steps on the left were the main entrance to the baths.

Scrap metal being cleared from Dewsbury Road on 11 September 1968. It was thrown out of an overturned lorry (shown in picture) belonging to Morley Waste Traders Ltd in a collision at the junction of Dewsbury Road with Moor Road. Two lorry drivers were taken to Leeds General Infirmary.

Myers and Co. (L&H) Ltd, 26 July 1968. The striking exterior of the newly acquired premises in York Place.

Weller Mount's old houses and the Scargill flats, 7 October 1968.

Council estate, Kirkstall, 12 October 1968.

Kelsall Road, one of the streets included in the modernisation scheme, on 22 October 1968.

Rodley, 1 November 1968. This is not a coastal view, but reflections of houses in the still waters of the Leeds and Liverpool Canal.

Children playing in Autumn Grove, one of the streets included in Leeds Corporation's modernisation plan for a 'twilight' area of the city, on 22 October 1968.

Armley, 15 January 1969. 'Today could have been the day an expanding Leeds firm began to move into its new premises. But instead they must be content to stand and admire its new building. For a one man men's hairdressing business in Armey Road, run by 46-year-old Mr Leslie Jackson is standing in the way. His shop – the only remainig old property in the middle of an Armley demolition area – stands a few feet in front of the firm's new premises, just where the forecourrt should be, partly blocking the warehouse entrance. "Until Mr Jackson moves out, we will not be able to move in," says the firm, Rothera and Brereton Ltd. paper merchants. For months Mr Jackson, who rents the shop from Leeds Corporation has been waiting for a new shop to be completed on the Theaker Lane Estate, Armley.'

Armley, 28 March 1969. Burnsall Grange flats in Theaker Lane, towering above older property in Town Street.

Seacroft village green, 1 July 1969.

Outside the Civic Hall on 23 July 1969. Demonstrating an 85ft fire escape (officially called an hydraulic platform), which had just been bought by the city's Fire Brigade.

E.P. Caseroom on Albion Street, 1 August 1969. 'And here is what we call a Linotype machine,' E.P. Deputy Caseroom Overseer George Bird tells Ulrike Rossler (seated), from Dortmund, Germany. Ulrike is the penfriend of George's daughter Alison (second left), and the other girls in the picture – Barbara Wilson and Janet and Elizabeth Wright – are some of Alison's Leeds friends. George treated them all to a behind the scenes glimpse of a newspaper.

Members of the Leeds Music Centre Jazz Group on 15 September 1969, soon to leave for Hungary to take part in a jazz festival, pictured during a rehearsal at the centre in Cookridge Street. From left to right: Mick Goodrick (bass), Malcolm Woodward (drums), Ray Manderson (trumpet), Dave Cliff (guitar), Bryan Layton (tutor), Joseph Stones (director) and Peter Welburn (tenor saxophone).

The golfhouse, Gott's Park, Armley, on 1 October 1969.

20 October 1969. Miss Linda Peel, of Gledhow, Leeds, tests her breath at a demonstration. A sweet which was claimed to effectively beat the breatalyser test without reducing the level of alcohol in the blood was demonstrated in Leeds to publicans and hoteliers. The sweet, developed by a German, was claimed to neutrilise the smell of tobacco, spicy foods, garlic, onions and alcohol. They cost 2s each and had a lime flavour.

Wortley, 16 December 1969. Mr Andrew Ross takes his daughter's baby for an outing down muddy Wheelwright Avenue, Lower Wortley. With him is two-year-old Colin Glacken who lives in the avenue.

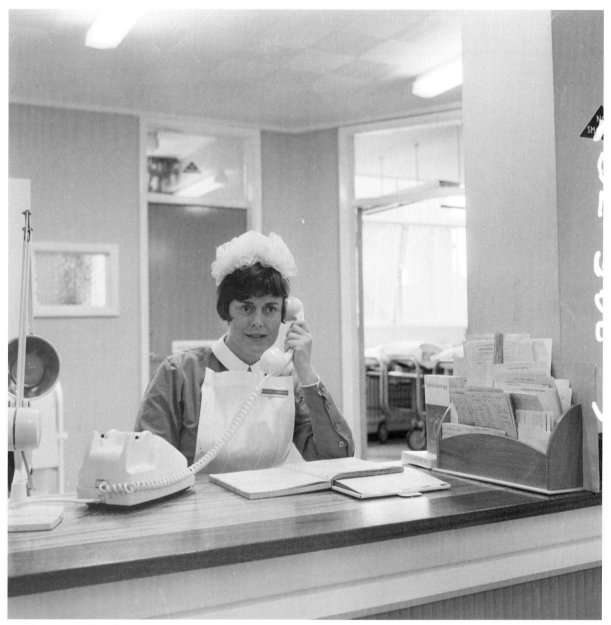

Leeds General Infirmary in 1969. Bi-Centenary Advert Feature.

The 1970s

Yvonne's, Beeston, in the 1970s.

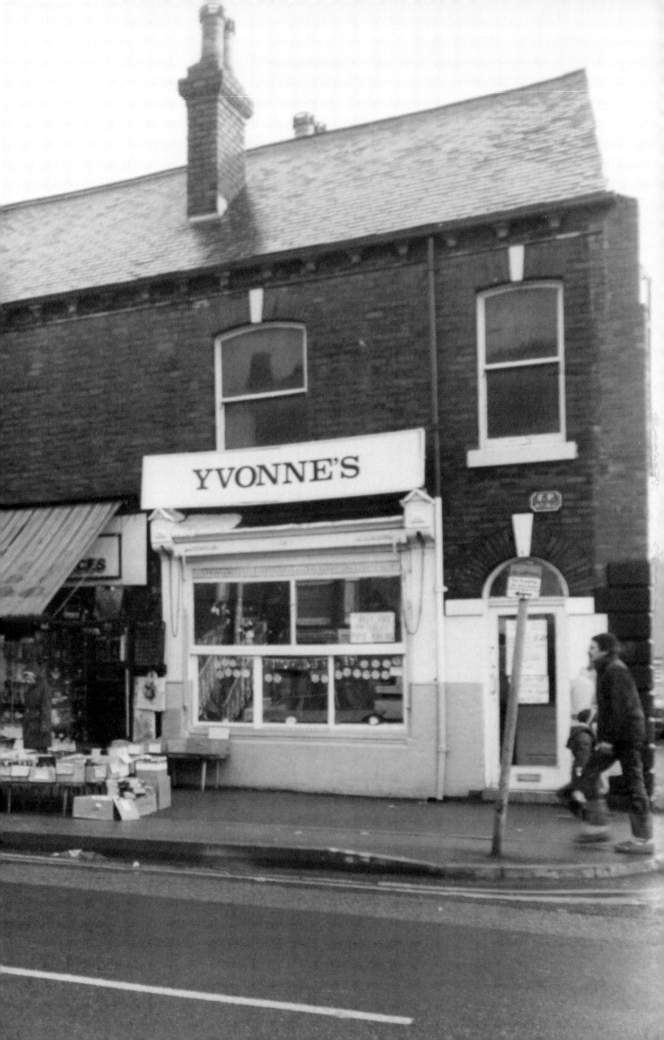

Horsforth, 12 January 1970. Horsforth Council's new refuse disposal plant. Mr Terry Finn was the tin baler of the pulverisation plant.

Alwoodley, 19 January 1970. In the Leeds suburb of Alwoodley, high hedges and trees shield the Corporation estate from view on the Nursery Lane border.

Pupils cross Headingley Lane on their way home from Leeds Girl's High School on 21 January 1970.

York Road, 27 January 1970.

Leeds Wholesale Market fish buyers place their orders in the fish market on 24 February 1970.

An early-morning buyer inspects turkeys in the poultry section of the market on 24 February 1970.

Farnley, 6 February 1970. Residents of the 'Mad Mile' area of Farnley read a new warning notice put up by Leeds City Police at the junction of Whincover Drive and Farnley Ring Road.

Seacroft Village Post Office on 20 March 1970.

A shopping parade in Roundhay Road photographed from Harehills Road on 29 April 1970.

1 June 1970. 'Miss Liz Hirst, aged 21, of Cardigan Road, Headingley, Leeds is seen examining today one of a number of notices which have been put up near the junction of Albion Street and Commercial Street, Leeds.

These notices spell out exactly what will happen in the Autumn when the area becomes part of a large pedestrian precinct, incorporating Bond Street, Commercial Street, King Charles Croft, King Charles Street and Lands Lane. All vehicles, apart from essential users such as fire appliances, ambulances and delivery vehicles, will be barred from the area between 10am and 6pm on all days except Sundays.'

The annual contest of the Ancient Silver Scorton Arrow at Adel Memorial Hall, Leeds on 5 July 1970. Drawing back his bow is Mr Ben Hird, the oldest living captain who won the Scorton Silver Arrow in 1900 at the age of 19. He competed again for the title at the age of 89.

Harehills, 8 August 1970. 'Two terrace houses in Harehills Place, Harehills, Leeds, vacant for nearly five years, may soon be made habitable again', said a spokesman for Leeds Corporation.

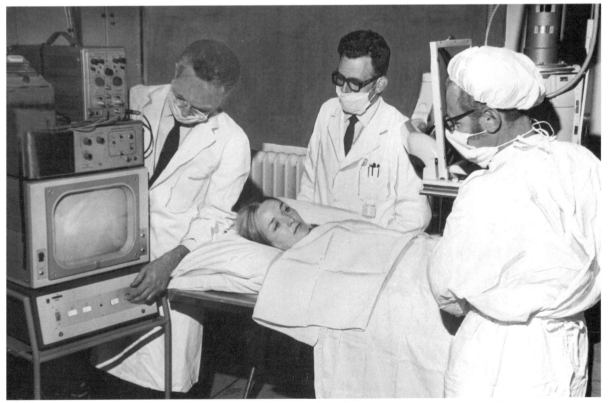

Demonstrating the new apparatus at Leeds General Infirmary on 10 August 1970.

West Riding police cars on 20 October 1970.

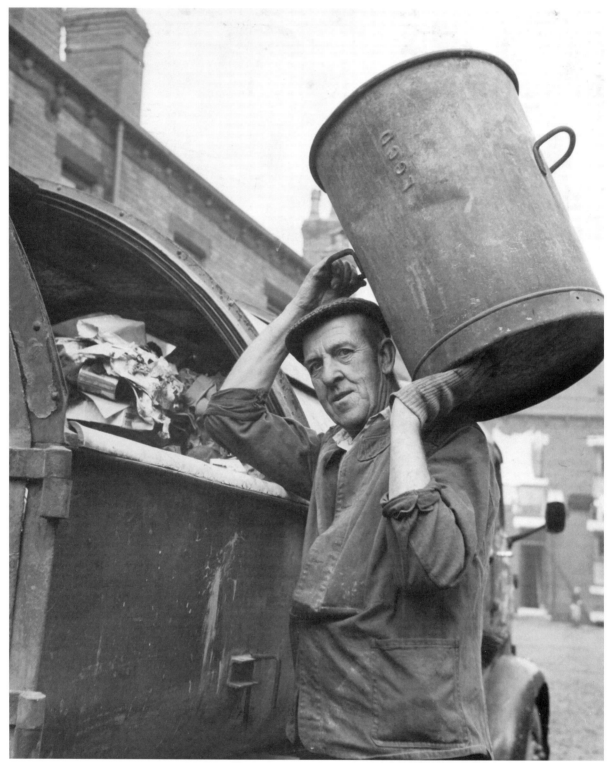

Mr Jim Whitehead (62), dustman for Leeds Corporation for 11 years, carrying a bin on 24 September 1970. His basic wage was £17 2s. He paid £4 6s 6d rent for his Corporation house in Rosedale Walk, Belle Isle, and other regular bills cost around £2 5s a week. He also had to provide boots and clothing for winter for what he described as a thankless job. 'Our leaders would have been better going in for £5 rather than 55s' he said. 'People have the idea we earn £20 a week. It is ridiculous'.

A view of the Wellington Street/Wellington Road junction on 16 October 1970.

The official tip near the Meanwood cricket ground on 1 November 1970.

Woodhouse Lane, 13 November 1970. 'England's oldest dispensing chemist, Mr Walter Thomas Castelow, aged 98. Mr Castelow who was always immaculately dressed in 19th-century style with a two inch high starched collar and polka dot cravat, first began working in the shop 67 years ago, he was still serving the public up to a week before his death. When he started his working life, Mr Castelow signed indentures as an apprentice at 2s 6d a week and gave a binding not to play dice, not to marry, not to haunt taverns or playhouses and not to absent himself from his masters service day or night, unlawfully. He was widowed 15 years ago and leaves two sons and two daughters.'

Pudsey, 10 December 1970. Children get a special off-schedule visit from the Prince of Wales outside Thornbury Barracks.

Noel Fashions on Lands Lane and Commercial Street corner on 27 January 1971. Lotus Shoes in background.

Snow in Leeds on 8 February 1971.

Stanningley Bypass, 22 March 1971. Taken from the Henconnor Bridge.

Stanningley Bypass, 22 March 1971. A view of a section of the Stanningley bypass looking towards Leeds from the bridge on Swinnow Road, Bramley.

1 May 1971. 'Actress Pat Phoenix autographs photographs in Leeds today. Pat Phoenix, the *Coronation Street* star, today opened a new department for women with fuller figures at a Leeds Store. Miss Phoenix, who wore a midi length sea green coat trimmed with mink collar and cuffs which she designed herself said: "I know I have this glamorous image but I like to dress to please myself." After opening the "44 Room" at Matthias Robinson store, Briggate, Miss Phoenix known to TV fans as Elsie Tanner for the last 10 years – spoke of the difficulties of pleasing fans, critics and herself when she bought clothes. "For quite some time I was a 44in hip," said Miss Phoenix as she sipped unsweetened coffee and refused fattening foods. "It was hard to find fashionable clothes for my figure in a fashion field which had long been neglected". Miss Phoenix has bought a pair of hot pants but with a cover up skirt. She thinks she is too old to show her legs.'

Elland Road, 17 April 1971. Police escort one of the sit-down protestors from the West Bromwich Albion goalmouth as 'keeper Cumbes walks past.

Elland Road, 17 April 1971. Spectators removed from the field during Leeds United v West Bromwich Albion match.

Billy Bremner Holds the trophy aloft after Leeds beat Juventus in the Inter-cities Fairs Cup Final on 3 June 1971.

17 June 1971. 'The corn dollies of Yorkshire are helping Miss Celia Gardiner gain her Master of Philosophy at Leeds University. In two years, from her research, she hopes to submit a thesis on corn dollies in the county to earn another degree to add to her Aberdeen University MA.'

Preparing joints in the butchery at Woolworth's Leeds store, 18 June 1971.

Mr Charles L'Anson (bottom left), a sculptor, helps workmen erect his Crucifixion figure at the chapel at Trinity and All Saint's Colleges, Horsforth, near Leeds on 13 October 1971. Using himself as a model, Mr L'Anson took 18 months to complete the bronze and glass fibre work. 'It has been made in the same way as fibre glass car bodies, exept that the shape has, of course made it complicated,' said Mr L'Anson, a senior lecturer in sculpture at the colleges.

Market stalls in Seacroft, 12 November 1971.

Far left: Old adverts from the *Yorkshire Evening Post*, 1972.

Left: Old adverts from the *Yorkshire Evening Post*, 1972. Including Plaza Cinema showing *Murders in the Rue Morgue,* and *The Return of Count Yorga.*

An old advert from the *Yorkshire Evening Post*. 'Factor For Men' cologne.

An old advert from the *Yorkshire Evening Post*. Isle of Man Tourism.

Pictured on the moors are these cadets of the Seacroft detachment of the Leeds Rifles, on 8 January 1972. From left to right: Brian Dickinson, Steven Dixon, Gary Spence and Danny McCraffrey.

Coal merchants collect fuel for priority domestic users at the Hargreaves wholesale depot at Marsh Lane on 21 January 1972. The yard had been closed since the previous Wednesday, and on 21 January NUM pickets allowed in the lorries after merchants promised only to deliver to pensioners and priority users.

View of the police check point on the York Road, near Gipton Police Station from 5 May 1972, where all vehicles leaving the city were searched.

Cottingley Heights Opening, 19 April 1972.

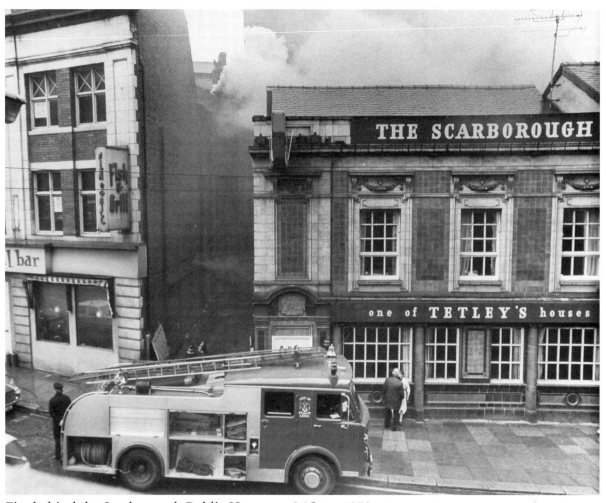

Fire behind the Scarborough Public House on 26 June 1972.

The new Bramley Middle School, Hough Lane, on 29 July 1972, one of the very few new buildings in the district.

The lions in front of Leeds Town Hall get a hosedown on 15 July 1972. This is to soften the stone for cleaning.

Youngsters crowd into the Youth Careers Office on 22 September 1972 to join the dole queue.

Dated 30 August 1972. Police issued a warning about the 'dangerous' practice of daubing slogans with sprays on motorway bridges. It came from West Yorkshire Police after the example (left) was found on a bridge over the M1 northbound carriageway at Stourton.

The exterior of Vallances showing the front entrance at the Corn Exchange on 16 November 1972.

The new pedestrian precinct near Vallences shop on the corner of Central Road and new Market Street and opposite the Corn Exchange on 16 November 1972. Vallances had cleaned the exterior of their building, transforming it from black to mellow red brick. Inside the ground floor had been completely refitted to provide better display facilities for the wide range of radio, TV, hi-fi and domestic appliances Vallences sold.

Street Lane, 23 November 1972. Leslie Harris thinks Barney Siddal is a cut above all the others. That is why he has given him his trade for nearly 18 years. And Barney (63), the barber of Street Lane, Leeds, knew it was a snip when he met Les and a touch of the best treatment started a long friendship. A quick reckoning by Leslie, managing director of a firm at Wyke, Bradford shows that he must have visited Barney for a haircut over 450 times. In these days of long hair for men, that is the sort of customer Barney wants.

Shops in Kippax High Street on 18 November 1972.

A section of the new South East Leeds motorway which was opened during the week of 11 December 1972 as part of the M1 construction.

Leeds South East Urban Motorway, Hunslet Road, 15 December 1972.

Children of the Women's Circle meet Charlie Cairoli at Leeds City Varieties during a production of the pantomime *Jack and the Beanstalk* on 9 January 1973. Pictured with the famous clown and Ann Langford.

Mrs Rose's shop in Oldfield Lane, Wortley, 31 January 1973, where an attack took place.

Methley Drive, off Harrogate Road, on 2 February 1973, with big family houses fitted with bay windows – many of the houses in this area were back-to-backs.

Pupils of the Leeds Free School reading comics on 5 February 1973.

One of the homely old streets of terraced houses on 1 March 1973.

Wellington Street, Northern Street Junction, dated 9 March 1973.

Part of the boarded up façade of the National Carriers Depot on 9 March 1973.

Wellington Street on 9 March 1973. The Post Office Tower is under construction on left.

Tetley Bittermen advertising billboard on Wellington Street, 9 March 1973.

Wellington Street, 9 March 1973.

Wellington Street, 9 March 1973.

Westgate, 30 April 1973.

The junction of Stanningley Road and Leeds and Bradford Road, 2 May 1973.

Boarded up council house, 69 Belle Vue Road on 9 August 1973.

Meanwood, 17 November 1973. Caretaker Mr Charles Matthews with some of the crates of milk bottles at St Thomas Aquinas School.

1 March 1973. 'Mr Albert Marshall, 62, who works as a general blacksmith in Goodman Street, Hunslet. "If I do not find anywhere else I will have to close down. As far as I know I am the only self-employed blacksmith left in Leeds." He said that he no longer shoed horses and that 50 per cent of his work was in making the iron framework to support gymnasium equipment.'

Speech Day at Leeds Grammar School, 25 October 1973. From left to right: Martin Francis (16), The View, Roundhay; Geoffrey Bellamy (18), Buckingham Road, Headingley; Chotai Sanjay (17), Cliffe House Avenue, Garforth; Robert Brakewell (11), Hartley Avenue, Woodhouse; Jonathan Harcourt (10), Linton Close, Wharfe Grove, Wetherby; Bob Nowill (17), Head Boy, Otley Road, Adel; Peter Levine (17), Deputy Head Boy, Wigton Lane, Alwoodley; Ian Bosley (18), Deputy Head Boy, of Lyndale, Kippax.

The Aladdin's Cave of the Post Office – Mr Clarence Bateman among the racks and racks of lost property at Quebec Street, 24 July 1973.

Benjamin Simons Clothing factory at the junction of Westgate and Park Lane on 19 January 1974.

The long, long queue for the two basins where 70 pupils of St Luke's Primary School must wash, 29 January 1974.

A typical shopper's-eye view of Scarrs in Leeds Market from 31 January 1974.

British Sub Aqua Club in Yorkshire treasure hunt in Waterloo Lake, Roundhay Park on 17 March 1974. Checking the equipment before making a dive are, from left to right: D. McIntyre, N. Hall, H. Pearson and D. Child, all members of the Leeds branch of the British Sub Aqua Club.

Members of the East Leeds Youth Orchestra with Mr Michael Landa (left), conductor of the recorder group, and Mr J. Renhard, the orchestra's conductor on 23 March 1974.

Photograph dated 22 July 1974 showing all that remains of the office effects from the fire-gutted warehouse in Marsh Lane. The men are employees of National Carriers Ltd, who had an office in the building.

Wellington Street, 26 July 1974.

A general view of part of the Tate Truck Centre in Balm Road on 24 September 1974.

Farnley, 7 January 1975. Mr Norma Lyons and his wife Sybil living in Long Row.

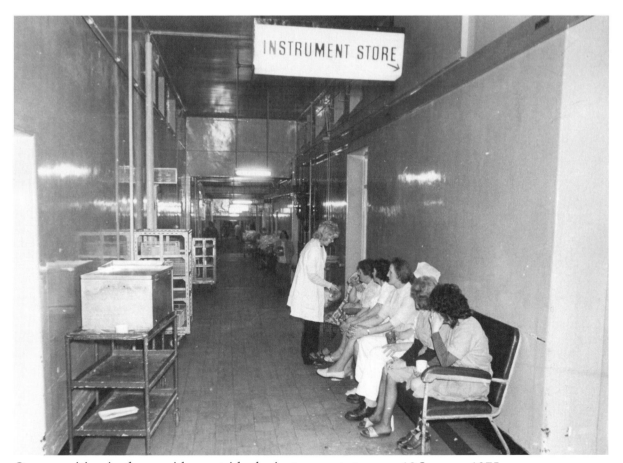

Queue waiting in the corridor outside the instrument store on 10 January 1975.

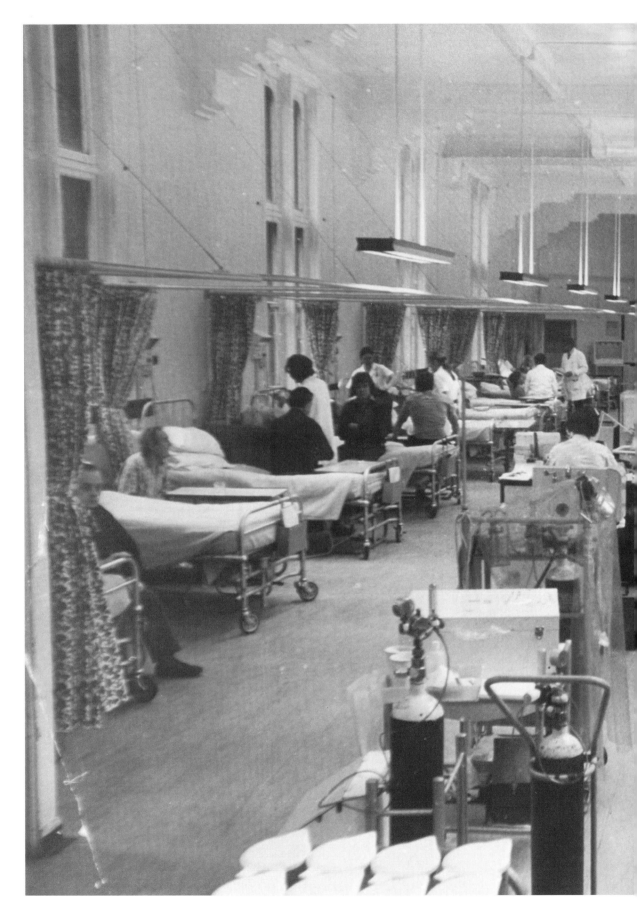

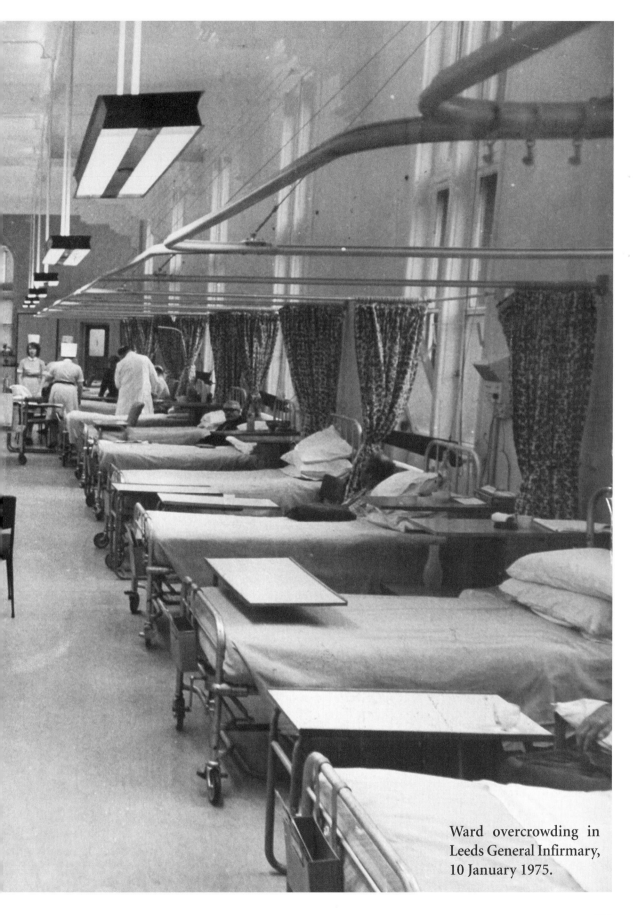

Ward overcrowding in Leeds General Infirmary, 10 January 1975.

The old warehouse block at 58 Wellington Street on 10 April 1975.

Billy Bremner as captain of Leeds United with Johann Cruyff, captain of Barcelona, during a European match on 9 April 1975.

A view of York Road from 13 May 1975 taken from the junction with Lupton Avenue and looking towards the Shaftesbury cinema.

The pedestrian footbridge over York Road at the junction of Harehills Lane on 21 July 1975.

Millionaire Manny Cussins outside one of his Leeds Stores on 10 June 1975.

Wellington Street, 6 August 1975. 'The first Leeds city-centre filling station for vehicles converted to run on petroleum gas has opened in Wellington Street, Leeds. Cargoes Cargas Ltd. has moved its filling point from Birkenshaw to a site in the old Central Station goods yard at the junction of Wellington Street and Queen Street. Mr Ray Hughes, managing director, explained. "We were desperate to get into Leeds city centre. Now we are able to offer a better service to fleet owners and private motorists who have had their cars converted." The filling station has a small tank which can easily be replenished every day from the company's larger installation at Ossett.'

The site in Vicar Lane on 22 September 1975 between Willis Ludlows store and the north door of the market which was to have been a multi-million-pound development.

Leeds University Rag Week. A big crowd watches Leeds students' rag procession move through the city centre on 30 November 1975.

The tree-lined Lidgett Park Road, Roundhay, 20 October 1975.

Bridge over the Harehills Lane–York Road junction on 13 November 1975.

Pudsey, 18 November 1975. 'Comedian Terry Scott who is to star as Dame in the Bradford Alhambra panto *Goldilocks and The Three Bears*, shares a joke when opening a bargain sale held by the Pudsey branch of the Save the Children Fund at the Unitarian Church, Pudsey.'

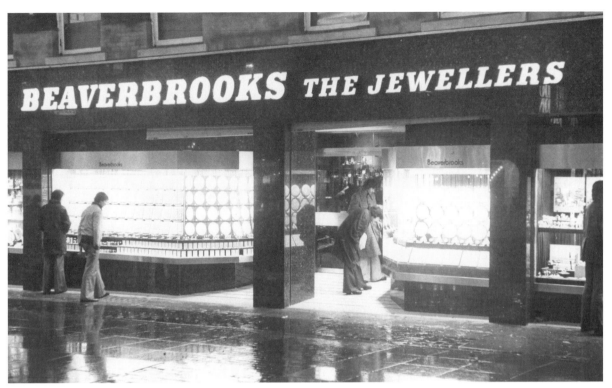

A view of Beaverbrooks Jewellers at night from 30 September 1975.

The bus lane in Water Lane, looking towards Victoria Road, on 4 December 1975.

Fire at Kirkgate Market on 13 December 1975. The photograph shows the blaze at its height.

Busy shoppers in Leeds Fruit and Vegetable Market, 23 December 1975.

A sign is nailed to the door of the old Millgarth Police Station on 14 January 1976 after the building finally closed.

Armley, 21 January 1976. 'Only a handful of folk still live in Sultan Street, Whingate Junction. The Redshaws, Cloughs, Lowes, Harkers and Ackroyds went long ago, but all their yesterdays are preserved in one house, No. 13. Behind the boards of No. 13 are the leaded windows of another era – restored by ITV for a school's history programme *How We Used to Live*.'

The Spencer sisters, Katie, six, and Sally, four, of Moor Flatts Road, Middleton, presenting flowers to singers Peters and Lee at Schofields store, Leeds on 22 May 1976.

Bass & Bligh Cameras and Binoculars' new premises in Lower Briggate on 25 October 1976.

Hyde Park, 11 May 1976. The house standing in the middle of the clearance area is the home of Mrs Emilia McCourt who were the only residents left in Howden Place.

The first public performance of Leeds United star Duncan McKenzie's 'party piece' of leaping over a mini car was seen at Elland Road before the Paul Reaney testimonial game on 3 May 1976.

Armley, 13 May 1977. Fitzarthur Street, Fearnley Street, Gledhow Street in Tong Road. A seventies action group tried to save them from demolition but were unsuccessful.

Headingley, 19 April 1977. A cheese and wine old time music hall evening organised by the Women's Fellowship in aid of Christian Aid was held at All Hallows Church, Headingley. Seen getting into the spirit of the evening is Mr Harry Lewis, tuning into an old phonograph, one of a collection by Mr David Trigg (right), who presented his *Clockwork Music Hall Road Show* at the evening. Also pictured are (from left): Mrs Alice Lewis, Mrs Peggy Bell and Mr Bill Bell.

Leeds schoolchildren at Bedford Field Middle School on 4 July 1977 rehearse the mass display of Scottish dancing which the Queen will see the following week.

Old advert for Wigfalls from the *Yorkshire Evening Post*, 1978.

Opposite: Old advert for Robert Bowett from the *Yorkshire Evening Post*, 1978.

Left: Old advert for Appleyard from the *Yorkshire Evening Post*, 1978.

Debenhams

Old advert for Debenhams from the *Yorkshire Evening Post*, 1978.

Old advert for Cox of Leeds from the *Yorkshire Evening Post*, 1978.

Now you can rent a colour set for the kitchen, bedroom, kids' room, living room, dining room –for £6·95 a month.

Brand new 14″ colour set, built-in aerial. Six months' advance rental, only £41.70 (Govt. regulation) no more for six months, then £6.95 a month. Minimum rental period one year. Backed by full expert D.E.R service, naturally.

DER

a million renters can't be wrong

Brand new from

Bingley 12 Myrtle Walk. Bingley 7141/2.   Castleford 58 Carlton Street. Castleford 553869/557836.
Cross Gates 48 Arndale Centre. Leeds 602118/9.   Dewsbury 26 Corporation Street. Dewsbury 466938.
Goole 66 Boothferry Road. Goole 2222.   Harehills 268 Harehills Lane. Leeds 626337.
Harrogate 35 Beulah Street. Harrogate 502427.   Headingley 27 North Lane. Leeds 755599.
Horsforth 51 Town Street. Leeds 586011.   Leeds Centre 93 Albion Street. Leeds 34176.
40 Commercial Street. Leeds 450458.   Pontefract 9 Ropergate. Pontefract 702499/703941.
Pudsey 11a Church Lane. Pudsey 561151.   Ripon 9 Fishergate. Ripon 3160.
Roundhay 248 Roundhay Road. Leeds 624768/9.   Selby 27 Finkle St. Selby 2746.
Wakefield 56 Upper Kirkgate. Wakefield 73858/9.   York 6 Feasegate. York 22582.

Old advert for DER from the *Yorkshire Evening Post*, 1978.

The 'Stay-awhile' ticket.

Monthly Return by Inter-City.

If you are planning to stay with relatives or friends, here is just the ticket for you.

The Monthly Return.

You can stay for up to a month, and you'll make a worthwhile saving.

The free booklet illustrated tells you how to choose and use the Fare Deal money-saving tickets – Awayday, Weekend, Monthly and Economy Returns. Get your copy from principal British Rail stations, Travel Centres or Travel Agents.

HOW TO CHOOSE YOUR RAIL TICKET and save money

Monthly Return Savings

Some 2nd Class fares from LEEDS

	Monthly Return	Saving on Standard Return
Blackpool	£5.86	£1.93
Bournemouth	£20.61	£5.55
Colwyn Bay	£9.33	£2.12
Edinburgh	£15.33	£5.10
London	£17.05	£3.40
Newquay	£25.70	£7.88

These fares cannot be used on certain trains — please check before booking. Half price for children aged 3 years and under 14; children under 3 years free. 1st Class Monthly Returns are also available.

Your local telephone enquiry number **Leeds 36163.**

Inter-City

Have a good trip!

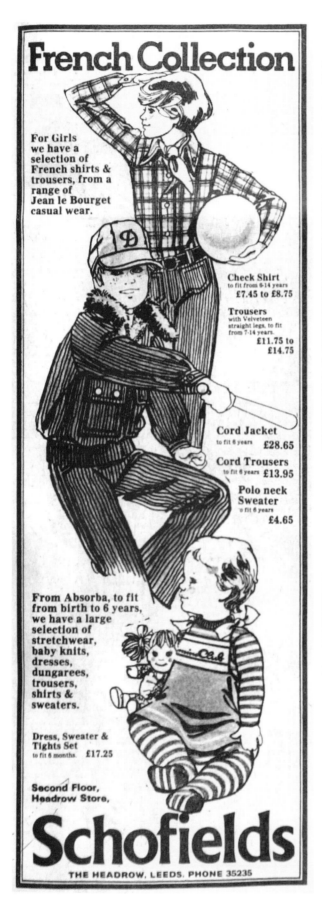

Old advert for Negas Avis *Evening Post* offer from the *Yorkshire Evening Post*, 1978.

Opposite: Old advert for Intercity from the *Yorkshire Evening Post*, 1978.

Old advert for Schofields from the *Yorkshire Evening Post*, 1978.

Old advert for Gratispool
from the *Yorkshire Evening
Post*, 1978.

Armley, 23 March 1978. Grasmere Street, one of the streets in the clearance area.

A picture of innocence? Robert Morley in his dressing room at the Grand Theatre, Leeds, on 19 May 1978.

Local Government Poll on 4 May 1978. A policeman on duty otside Royal Park Middle School polling station at Burley.

Back Room Service, 25 April 1978. Part of Vallences comprehensive workshops at Bramley, providing expert service back-up for their customers

Nos. 30 and 32 Bayswater Crescent, Harehills, 3 July 1978.

Armley, 23 May 1978. Middle Cross Street in the clearance area.

SIMPSON STREET

The packed snow on the road in Wellington Street on 27 January 1979.

The snow lashes down on people queuing for a bus to transport them home as the city evening rush hour begins in Boar Lane, 15 February 1979.

Dancing was once frowned upon in Methodist circles. Members of Newbourne Methodist Chapel, Richmond Hill, are glad those days are gone, as this picture from 2 March 1979 shows, for they are throwing tradition to the wind and earning a reputation for miles around for lively dances.

Firemen fight the blaze at L. Thackray and Sons, Engineers, Marsh Lane on 10 May 1979.

Bramley shopping centre, 4 December 1979.

Armley town centre, 4 December 1979.